TROMBONE

Wedding Essentials

CONTENTS

This book is arranged for 2 B-flat trumpets, French horn, trombone, and tuba. The music in this book is from the personal library of Canadian Brass and has been performed and recorded by Canadian Brass.

Other books from Canadian Brass

Book of Beginning Quintets	Play Along with Canadian Brass (easy level)
Book of Easy Quintets	Play Along with Canadian Brass (intermediate)
Book of Favorite Quintets (intermediate)	Canadian Brass Christmas Carols
Book of Advanced Quintets	Hymns for Brass
On Broadway	Immortal Folksongs
Rodgers and Hammerstein	Favorite Classics

Visit *www.canadianbrass.com* for recordings from Canadian Brass

HAL•LEONARD®
CORPORATION
7777 W. BLUEMOUND RD. P.O. BOX 13819 MILWAUKEE, WI 53213

Visit Hal Leonard online at
www.halleonard.com

"AIR"
from *Water Music*

Handel
(1685-1759)
Arranged by Walter Barnes

LARGO

from *Xerxes*

3

George Frideric Handel
(1685-1759)
arranged by Walter Barnes

TROMBONE

PRAYER

from *Hansel and Gretel*

TROMBONE

Engelbert Humperdinck
(1854-1921)
arranged by Henry Charles Smith

AIR ON THE G STRING
from Suite No. 3

Trombone

J. S. Bach
(1685–1750)
Trans. by A. Frackenpohl

CANON

Johann Pachelbel
(1653-1706)
arranged by Walter Barnes

TROMBONE

FANFARE
from ORFEO

Trombone

Claudio Monteverdi
(1567-1643)
adapted and arranged by Stephen McNeff

Fine

Da Capo al Fine

rit.

TRUMPET TUNE AND AYRE

Henry Purcell
(1659-1695)
arranged by Walter Barnes

TROMBONE

TRUMPET VOLUNTARY

Stanley
(1713-1786)
arranged by Walter Barnes

Trumpet Voluntary *continued*

TRUMPET VOLUNTARY

Jeremiah Clarke
(1673-1707)
arranged by Walter Barnes

TROMBONE

BRIDAL CHORUS
from LOHENGRIN

Richard Wagner
(1813-1883)
edited by Canadian Brass

Trombone

WEDDING MARCH

Trombone

Felix Mendelssohn
(1809–1847)
Adapted by Ryan Anthony

RONDEAU
(Theme from *Masterpiece Theatre*)

TROMBONE

Jean-Joseph Mouret
(1682-1738)
arranged by Walter Barnes

OTHER APPROPRIATE WEDDING PIECES

Prelude
Fantasie (Bach)
Sheep May Safely Graze (Bach)*
Where e'er you walk (Handel)*

Prelude or Solo
Bist du bei mir (Bach, attr.)

Prelude or Processional
Jesu, Joy of Man's Desiring from *Cantata 147* (Bach)
Wachet auf (Sleepers Awake) from *Cantata 140* (Bach)*

Processional or Recessional
Trumpet Voluntary (Boyce)
Prelude from *Te Deum* (Charpentier)
March (Allegro spiritoso) from *Heroic Suite* (Telemann)

Solo
Ave Maria (Bach/Gounod)
Ave Maria (Schubert)

Recessional
Ode to Joy (Beethoven)
Allegro from *Water Music* (Handel)*
Arrival of the Queen of Sheba from *Solomon* (Handel)*
La Rejouissance (The Rejoicing) from *Music for the Royal Fireworks* (Handel)

More Recommended Music for Weddings
My heart ever faithful from *Cantata 68* (Bach)
Pavane (Fauré)
Pie Jesu from *Requiem, Op. 48* (Fauré)
Panis Angelicus (Franck)
Let the Bright Seraphim from *Samson* (Handel)*
Psalm XIX: The Heavens Declare (Marcello)
Toccata (Martini)
Alleluia from *Exsultate, jubilate* (Mozart)*
Ave verum corpus (Mozart)*
Agnus Dei (Palestrina)
Sonata for Two Trumpets and Brass (Purcell)*
Concerto in C (Vivaldi)*

*Canadian Brass publications